Don't Expect Much

Texts by Dr Stephen Bury, Martin Herbert

Introduction by Alistair Robinson
Additional contributions by Martin Clark, Deborah Kermode,
Hugh Mulholland and Stuart Tulloch

Northern Gallery for Contemporary Art.

First published by Northern Gallery for
Contemporary Art in 2004, with Ormeau Baths
Gallery, in an edition of 1000.

Northern Gallery for Contemporary Art,
City Library and Arts Centre, Fawcett Street,
Sunderland, SR1 1RE

http://www.ngca.co.uk
ngca@sunderland.gov.uk

Edited and co-ordinated by Alistair Robinson
at Northern Gallery for Contemporary Art.
Catalogue design by Paul Hetherington.
Printed in the UK by Field Print.

Accompanies a touring project organised by
Northern Gallery for Contemporary Art with
Ormeau Baths Gallery, Herbert Read Gallery, Kent
Institute of Art and Design, The Grundy Art Gallery,
Blackpool and Ikon, Birmingham, and generously
supported by Arts Council England.

ISBN 0-9549119-0-3

With thanks to:
Roel Arkesteijn, The Brothers, Jason Brown, Kadar
Brock, Stephen Bury, Martin Clark at Herbert Read
Gallery, Tom and Laurie Clarke, Gordon Dalton,
Fletcher Gallery Services, Hannah Firth at Chapter,
Levin Haegele, Martin Herbert, Paul Hetherington,
Alexis Hubshman & Peter Ted Surace at Rare Gallery,
Deborah Kermode at Ikon, Mark Jenkins at K2, Bob
Jones, Alistair Hudson and Penny Johnson at the
Governement Art Collection, Mr and Mrs Mackay,
William Ling, Hugh Mulholland at Ormeau Baths
Gallery, Samantha Peace at Arts Council North East,
Matthew Rowe at Towner Gallery, Alex Ryley, Dean
Turnbull, Katy Cole, Hannah Parsonage, Jane
Peverley at Northern Gallery for Contemporary
Art, Richard Salmon, Paul Stolper, Sally Townsend
at The Multiple Store, Stuart Tulloch at The Grundy
Art Gallery, Emma Underhill and Gemma de Gruz
at UP Projects, Liz Ward at London Institute, Louise
Wright at the British Council. Gary Arber, Stephen
Little.

With special thanks to Cassie Liversidge.

What You'd Expect

Peter Liversidge

Introducing
Peter Liversidge

Text by Alistair Robinson
Programme Director, Northern Gallery
for Contemporary Art

Over the last decade, Peter Liversidge's work has encompassed almost every medium and mode of address available to artists today. Creating paintings, drawings, sculptures, installations, multiples, videos, and works realised in the public realm, the artist has avoided a 'signature' motif or style in order to allow every avenue of investigation into his chosen subjects to remain open. Liversidge's *modus operandi* is best characterised as an ongoing investigation – through every means possible – into two twinned mythologies. These are respectively the ideology which provides luxury consumer goods with their status and desirability, and our imaginary representations of the American West. Rather than being driven by the use of a particular medium, the artist approaches these two mythologies from every conceivable angle, uniting them through his own distinctive working method and aesthetic. For several years, for example, he has been creating two ongoing series' of paintings which depict near-cinematic American landscapes, and a second appropriating famous brand logotypes.

In the former series, the vastness of the North Montana Plains is conveyed through unexpected disjunctures of scale. At first glance, the works are innocent, romanticized views of broad expanses of prairie and sky, suggesting glorious homages to the American West. Their two-colour ultra-simplified compositions manage to suggest both infinite pictorial depth and a flattened-out abstraction reminiscent of Alex Katz or Richard Diebenkorn. The horizon line, mostly set two-thirds of the way down each picture, conjures the gigantic skies of the plains – but in the most blissfully innocent way possible. After being drawn off-guard by the overwhelming élan of such works, more complex trains of thought begin to emerge.

Each of Liversidge's landscapes contain specks – but only specks – of narrative incident, usually drawn to our attention by the works'

[1]*Artforum, Feb 2002*

ominous and allusive titles. In 'All is Quiet on the North Montana Plains', herds of stampeding buffalo become simply tiny dots marked with legs, thundering across an otherwise empty landscape. Elsewhere, minuscule V-shaped brushmarks which punctuate the washes of blue sky stand in for giant buzzards preying on smaller animal life. Closer inspection reveals that each species is carefully individualised – buffalo are dark brown dashes; predatory wolves are soft grey streaks; majestic elk are softer brown shades. Nothing here remains benign, and the grandeur and serenity of the natural wilderness is, in the most subtle and unexpected way, revealed to be a deception or idle fantasy.

Encountering Liversidge's paintings and sculptures, the viewer intuitively identifies a set of values and received ideas, only to have them undercut or re-oriented. In recreating found images – globally renown logotypes, for example – within his own, idiosyncratically hand-made idiom, the artist gently deflates the myths associated with them. As critic Dan Fox has written: "Liversidge's paintings are aspirational, yet their upwardly mobile ambitions are thwarted by their own clunky materiality. Liversidge celebrates the limits of his technical skill in order to debase the absurd levels of value and status ascribed to luxury products."

When examining consumer goods, Liversidge has recreated hundreds of logotypes, as though cataloguing every instance where advertising and branding have come to saturate our imagination and way of viewing the world. He has also created clunkily constructed simulacra of the appurtenances of the international tourist – such as American Express cards, 35mm cameras, and videocameras. It's easy to be taken in by the charm of such works, as Liversidge's take on the world can at first appear good humoured, or even cheerful. All of the artist's work possesses this persuasive and double-edged quality, which lulls us into a somewhat false sense of security.

The ostensible light-heartedness of the artist's approach can easily blind us to Liversidge's critical intent. Celebrating the bathetic has become, for him, a distinctive and novel way with which to dissect the processes with which we give order to the material world. Rather than adopting either the cool didacticism or provocative gestures of previous generations, the artist's working methods are disarming, gently highlighting the absurdity and contradictions of our collective comedy of category errors. Deflating the special status we accord to luxury goods by making unique works of art from them, is, as the artist is fully aware, an inherently contradictory enterprise. In Dan Fox's words, wittily anthropomorphising Liversidge's productions, "their upwardly mobile aspirations are thwarted by their own clunky materiality". By playing dumb, as it were, Liversidge leaves his own position ambiguous. His recreations of corporate interests' means of persuasion test how they personalise and provide a system of credence to mass-produced goods.

Critic Mason Klein has perhaps best encapsulated the artist's elliptical intentions with regards to his consumer goods series: "Liversidge's deliberately amateurish recycling of well-known, meticulously designed and crafted objects and glossy advertisements degrades the products and their insignia, negating their consumerist appeal and our now automatic associations of quality and reliability. Perfection is scarcely the objective. Liversidge's paintings and sculptures aim precisely to undermine advertising's crisp sheen. In reproducing internationally known signifiers like the logos of Lufthansa and BMW with a childlike clumsiness that strips all slickness from the corporate icons, the artist makes no bones about his apparently limited skill as a draughtsman: 'I really am trying … but I just can't paint these products the way the manufacturers would like to see them.'"[1]

Boulders, rocks and stones, V. 2002–03

The West:
A Visitors Guide

Text: Martin Herbert

Flip one of Peter Liversidge's paintings over and this is what you'll see. The title – 'the evil twister does its maiming and killing on the North Montana Plains', to take one juicy example from 1999 – handwritten using a black Rotring pen. And, beside it, the artist's name and the date upon which the painting was made, impersonally produced with a custom-made rubber-stamp. Since the date given is almost always a single day, and furthermore since the paintings themselves sometimes appear to have taken scant minutes of that given day to bring off, one reading of Liversidge's autographic style might be that he has little patience, either, with the niceties of self-identification. This would be a mis-conception. There's very little, if anything, that's slapdash about his work; or rather one could say that there is a theoretical meticulousness to even its most uncontrolled aspects and, consequently, not much about it that doesn't in some way signify in tandem with his larger project. The idea of the script and the rubberstamp, the mortal and the mechanistic and what their interlacing might mean, is sunk so deeply into Liversidge's art that it's present even where your eyes don't usually go.

Which might initially be hard to discern, looking at the *front* of the aforementioned '...evil twister...', a single rivulet from the stream of superficially similar images of the North Montana Plains – an American wilderness which Liversidge has never visited and whose topography and events he approximately invents – which he has produced since the late '90s. Blue skies and green swards proliferate here, painted wet-in-wet in watercolour. There is space aplenty to dream oneself into the landscape, as the eye, wishing to believe and to travel, enthusiastically compensates for informational lacunae created by the painting process and as felicities of drying paint, maximised in Liversidge's work via increasingly stern self-editing, suggest half-glimpsed geographical details. But there is also more than initially meets that eager optic: microscopic speckles of black and brown in the air and on the land, players in a tragic theatre of nature. As many of the titles make clear ('Dependent on Fresh Spring Growth, Elk Wander Across the North Montana Plains', 2004; 'Buzzards Enjoy the Warm Air Current over the North Montana Plains', 2001, for example), dynamism, fear and imminent demise routinely ricochet around these big horizons: the hunter and the hunted, both parties menaced by unpredictable weather and tough geography. This fact boosts the images way out of the sphere of the bucolic. Inevitably there is also the spectre of the Indian tribes – Blackfeet, Cheyenne,

Crow and others – who used to hunt buffalo all over the real Plains to which these are symbolic cousins. Though beautiful, these lands are also a succession of historical killing floors. City-dwellers turning to such paintings as de-stressors might find narrative elements in them surprisingly analogous to their own urbanite experience, whose punitive intensity is itself emphasized by the ubiquitous desire to escape from it.

Over the years, Liversidge's flat Montana has increasingly begun to jump off the wall, elements of it appearing as sculptural addenda: forked lightning bolts in painted wood; animal carcasses in various materials; wooden fences; and, perhaps most notably, fake rocks and boulders. The latter are made in a singularly mindless fashion; from balls of packing materials covered in brown masking tape. Piled up in galleries in a huge diversity of scales – pea-sized to towering – they are about belief and desperation, in a way; they test how much viewers wish to squint in order to place themselves far, far away from their usual surroundings, inserting themselves into a pastoral *mise-en-scène*. They are also the fruits of a microcosmic industry. Working with an assistant, Liversidge estimates that he can produce a couple of hundred of these things a day. They

embody a certain kind of monotonous, non-creative productivity, the sort of project that artists like to have on the go for the moments when inspiration might fail them (and there are certain artists whose genius resides in having their *entire practice* revolve around such piecework). But there is a danger in it; for when the work is done and installed as a totality it's hard for the viewer not to entertain fleeting thoughts, for good or ill, of the production line itself, which may have a detrimental effect on one's admiration for the art. In this body of work, however, that effect is not only accounted for but capitalized on. These things are constructed to deliver a fragile illusion; when the fantasy swiftly shatters, the labour is still glaringly evident. So the mind does move back, in turn, to the idea of these archetypes of the natural world rolling off a conveyor belt; but there's a structural reason for this equation of boulder country, where there's not much sustenance, with industrial production. Before we hunker down and get to it, we might be as well to cast a quick glance up to the ceiling and see if any buzzards are circling overhead.

Think about the millennia-old ubiquity of hunters and victims, and it would seem that we are not too far from cracking the central nut of Liversidge's art; to wit, why

he devotes significant periods of time to making images which seem to be of the natural landscape and much of the rest to plunging into the throbbing heartland of the commercial world via a steady output of images of corporate logos and advertisements, painted as if with the delirium tremens or, at least, a kind of nervous excitement. Because there is a why, and a better one than that increasingly popular among contemporary artists: that is, the simulation of a higher significance through a divergent practice which, in the final analysis, enigmatically refuses to hang together. That's not the situation here, and in fact closure is easier than it seems; you just have to stop looking at what the things are, and consider the common symbolic relations within them.

This can be done in various ways. Aside from noting that the luxury goods he enumerates and the class of wild landscape he imagines have a shared locus in Liversidge's trusty *National Geographic* magazines, the most superficial way of joining the dots – of avoiding the idea that there is, at most, simply a dialectic here, designed to make two discrete series of work shine through contrast – would be to bring the landscapes and logos together under the shared trope of *desire* as it

Montana. Ed. 3, 2001

mechanically plays itself out in the advanced-capitalist world: the figured wish for flight into product-lust or open space caused by the imprecations of urban life. This is a fair point, within limits. In Liversidge's case, the physical act of painting and drawing the heraldry of consumer items equates to a virtual caressing of carefully crafted logotypes, a touch which deforms as it goes; but which has the prospective effect of allowing the inscriber to know the topic entirely, because s/he has to paint it entirely. Or appears to allow, because there is a condition of disconnection here: just as painting a corporate logo won't get you the product, so ownership of the product won't finally allow you that dissolution into it, that ultimate identification with it, which is the subtext of all product-fetish and the goal of its advertising. This, naturally, is why Liversidge has often titled his advertisement paintings and drawings, with some degree of ironic bemusement, after the slogans that accompany the works. Examples: 'Now You Can Change Your Environment Without Changing Your Tyres', 1999; 'Do You Believe in the Power of Dreams?', 2004. Put these together with Liversidge's enthusiastic demolition of clean-lined design, and the figured breach is as broad as the Grand Canyon.

Still, as these artworks relay, the condition of ownership is additionally full of weird switchbacks between domination and being dominated, between liking and fearing both. In the paintings' own imperfection, first of all, is apparently a semi-vindictive wish to make the originals imperfect: to close the gap between the ideal, as figured in the advertisement, and the experience. This is something that's become increasingly clear in the recent large paintings Liversidge has made of international Olympic logos, which co-opt the Games' aspirational presentation of physical perfection; their twisting together of nationhood and idealism and Darwinism. Particularly in the case of those iconic interlinked rings but also in general, the logotype stands for the unattainable, and once you've either been kicked out of the gym for incompetence or unwrapped the product, waited for the spark, and remained inexplicably unchanged, it's hard to feel fully innocent again – until the next time you're feeling susceptible, of course …

On the other hand, there are definite consolations inherent in the time spent subsequently 'getting to know' whatever consumer product you thought would fill the void. A deformed logo echoes the idea of the impersonal being made yours, just as every pop and scratch on a vinyl record

proclaims its uniqueness and relation to you: your copy is unlike anyone else's, and you made it that way. Ditto the scuffs and scrapes on a camera's casing, which find themselves analogized, somehow, in the rough cardboard Leicas and Canons which Liversidge makes. And so there are solaces to be found on the level of personal engagement with the impersonal object, but you have to put them there yourself (notice, for example, how a worn second-hand disc sounds different to one you've wrecked yourself); and it's very hard, once you notice it, to escape that whole idea of the individual versus the mass miasma in Liversidge's work. Just as, once you see them in short succession, it's hard to avoid comparing a massive glut of advertising logos arranged willy-nilly on four walls with an avalanche of boulders and pebbles.

Some of Liversidge's logos are boulder-sized in terms of their underwritten corporate heft. Some are mere pebbles, like that of the place where the artist likes to get his bacon sandwiches, which by rights shouldn't even have a logo but, due to the owners' giddy wish to compete, does; and a nice one, too. But they're all out there on the flat plain, fighting for your attention. (Try and decide who to identify yourself with: the menaced buffalo or elk which might, nevertheless, have a chance of getting away from the circling birds of prey; or the desperate carrion bird which, if it doesn't find some sustenance soon, will drop out of the bright blue sky. If you identify with the evil twister, seek professional help.) This realm of fluent and multifarious metaphorical exchange extends beyond the viewer, however, and if one can associate the spread of logotypes in the built-up world with a mass of boulders, it may help also to map the practices of the bird of prey onto intentions of those corporations whose logos we see here. Rather than simply sitting there like a rock, each recognizable design has already fought its own battles to survive, and has come out on top. Otherwise, we wouldn't recognize it so easily, even mangled as it inevitably is here.

Furthermore, Liversidge's art suggests, this stuff is unequivocally *out there*, there's no going back now; and given that the wilderness is as brutal and basic as the city, all one can do is negotiate with it and forego romantic illusions. Thus, and in the manner which Chekhov advised all artists to follow, he isn't so much identifying putative answers so much as trying to clarify a problem as sharply as possible – in his case, a problem with the incomplete nature of selfhood and its easeful manipulation from outside or above.

But the works he produces when he's not following either of these twin (and, as we've seen, intertwined) strands are notable in their presentation of an alternative social system based on gifts and spontaneous irruptions in the bland fabric of the everyday, to the point where they appear hesitantly to edge toward a better, or at least less avaricious modality of being. On my desk, for instance, is a stack of 24 crisply minimal, beautifully printed postcards – collectively entitled '24 Days', sent to me by Liversidge on key dates from the beginning of 1999 to the start of 2000, and part of an edition of 10. Nearby is the corner of a wooden picture-frame, painted gold, whose thunderous arrival through my letterbox jerked me out of bed early one morning. I'm far from the only person to have received work through the post by him; notoriously, he's sent an egg, stamped and delivered intact, and a dismembered chair, piece by piece, through the British mail. There's something almost taboo about gifting: it goes against the profit motive. But then, Liversidge often seems to look bemusedly at consumerism's inbuilt obsolescence, as might be suggested equally by his recent films of antique toy bears and his long-term inability – since rectified, it appears – to use any more modern system of communication than a manual typewriter. Meanwhile, a certain bemusement at advanced capitalism's keenness to sell *anything* hums through in an editioned series, from 2001, of t-shirts bearing the legend 'I ❤ NMP' – the latter acronym standing, inevitably, for 'North Montana Plains'.

Pond. 2000. Folded restaurant napkins

One of Liversidge's early series was entitled 'Objects Made at Work Whilst I Should've Been Working', 1997–99, and consisted of beautifully carved and sanded items in a presentation case. The point, pretty clearly, was a circumvention of labour time within an acknowledgement of its inescapability; and an implicit suggestion that perhaps people should be allowed, and maybe even paid, to do what they're blatantly good at. That kind of pokey opposition to the invisible norm needs to be borne in mind when considering Liversidge's generous side-salad of public events; from the bright yards of bunting he's hung outside exhibitions to the hot-dog stand he's often set up and served free food out of, to the editioned posters he gives away at talks and the myriad public events planned in Birmingham, in collaboration with the Ikon Gallery, for this exhibition's tour, prospectively including a display of falconry; a 30ft tall, mobile, inflatable buffalo carcass; and the handing-out of a free, self-compiled CD.

What's perhaps most important to note, in an era where attempts to make art that has direct socio-political agency seem doomed from the start to preach to the choir, is that there's absolutely nothing polemical about all of this. Liversidge does

not progress from ideology to illustrative action but from non-illustrative (and, occasionally, demonstrably baffling) action to thought-stimulus, thereby delivering the favourable impression that, first, you constellated his rangy practice yourself and drew intelligent conclusions; and, second, that the artist was smart enough to create the means to let you. Yes, it's possible to pick and choose from his output. On occasion, surely, people have admired and/or bought his paintings of Cartier's logo for the same reasons of reflected glamour that they've admired and/or bought a Cartier watch. Others may simply wish to appreciate the thread of bemused humour that runs through his wonky pictorial gambits. But, take it in its entirety, and what emerges is a kind of – well, grand is never the right word for Liversidge's atomized, unshowy work, but, say, *cumulative* intensity of purpose which communicates plenty about the way we live our lives now or, more often, elect to let others live them for us. For navigational assistance, turn to the back of the painting.

What
You'd Expect

An elk corpse slides easily over the frozen wastes of the North Montana Plains. 8 July 2000. 32.1 x 31.9cm. Watercolour, emulsion, MDF

Edge of a forest. 2 January 2003. 37.8 x 27.5cm
Watercolour, emulsion, found wood. *Private Collection, London*

Forest at dawn. 25 April 2003. 68.8 x 50.8 cm. Watercolour, emulsion on found board. *Towner Gallery, Eastbourne*

The West. Installation, Richard Salmon Gallery, 2003

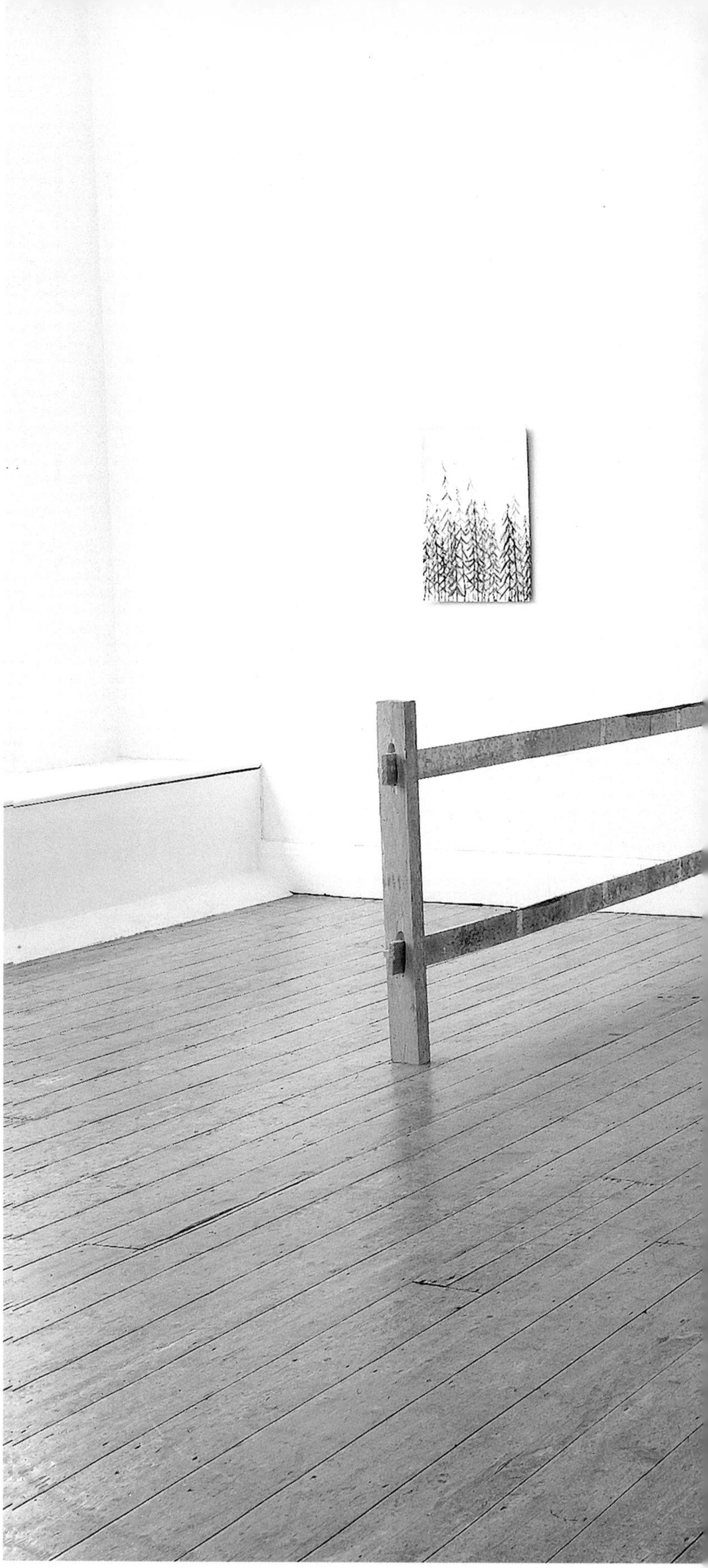

Fence. 2001

Carcasses. *The West*, installation, Richard Salmon Gallery, 2003

Western Country, installation Rare, New York, 2003

Lightning I. 1999

Paintings and sculpture. Installation, Rare, New York. 2001

The evil twister does its maiming and killing on the North Montana Plains. 3 May 1999. 17.5 x 18.5cm. *Private collection, London*

Midnight on the North Montana Plains. 15 July 1999. 19.1 x 22.3cm

All is quiet on the North Montana Plains. 30 December 2001. 37.7 x 40cm.

Elk consider the dangers faced in crossing the North Montana Plains. 22 April 2001. 29.4 x 31cm

In the distance eagles cry on the North Montana Plains. 15 August 2003. 38.2 x 40cm

Elk relax in the beauty of their surroundings on the North Montana Plains. 2003. 39 x 40 cm . *Private collection, London*

'A Story Told in the Eighth Person.'

Edited transcripts from a round-table discussion between the curators of project venues, conducted during late 2004.

Martin Clark, *Exhibitions Curator,* Herbert Read Gallery, Kent Institute of Art & Design

Deborah Kermode, *Curator (Off-site),* Ikon, Birmingham

Hugh Mulholland, *Director,* Ormeau Baths Gallery, Belfast

Alistair Robinson, *Programme Director,* Northern Gallery for Contemporary Art, Sunderland

Stuart Tulloch, *Curator,* The Grundy Art Gallery, Blackpool

AR— One issue which has struck me when seeing Peter's shows has been the problem of how, as an artist, you can forge a distinctive way of working which is uniquely your own. How do you offer the viewer a glimpse into a unique imaginary world? When there are hundreds of shows on at any given time, how do you carve out a convincing narrative about your own work, from nothing? Peter's answer to this seems to me to have been to constantly create images and objects – whenever and however – using the means required for the job. What unites his various activities and keeps them intriguing seems to be his generous, quixotic approach, and that allows his work to continually offer surprises.

ST— This seems a far more open-ended and dynamic approach to making work than trying to develop a 'unique selling proposition', say, which a number of artists fall into the trap of. I think that, during the '90s, so much new work was dependent upon employing gratuitous expense or stopping the viewer in their tracks with spectacle or overt displays of technical skill. Peter's work is never spectacular, nor driven by technique alone, nor about identifying himself with a particular material or selling proposition. Maybe this is a generational issue.

AR— Actually, when you know Peter's work you can identify common themes and ideas which link the diversity of his different activities. But you can honestly say that you can never be sure what his next work is going to look like, and that's quite something.

MC— There's certainly a world of difference between Peter's work and the way a previous generation traded off references to minimalism or through tactics of provocation. Certainly Peter's work wouldn't be described as 'dissenting' or 'transgressive', but it's all the more interesting because of the complexity of his relationship to the subject matter, the area of investigation. Popular culture may (mostly) still be the starting point, but Peter has neither a Warholian blankness nor a Barbara Kruger-let's-get-serious attitude.

DK— I think of Peter's work as being softly spoken, very quietly analytical. It provides a new viewpoint on the world of the signs we live in, through new or at least unexpected means, rather than mounting an overt critique or being part of a strategy of oppositionality. The times when artists became successful first and foremost by demonstrating their theoretical prowess or erudition are a little distant now. The primary characteristics of Peter's work seem to me to be inclusivity, generosity, and humour. But each work seems to be evidence of a freewheeling imagination and a sharp wit, too.

HM— I first became aware of Peter's work when he was selected for 'Perspective', an annual open exhibition held at OBG. His submission for this show exemplified the humour inherent in the work: he posted a multiple series of badly typed, unrealizable proposals for the space, ranging from a petting zoo in gallery one to a fully operational 'Kwik Fit' garage in gallery three. There is always a sense of the absurd about the work, and I love the way Peter is so earnest about it all. You're standing looking at one of the Montana paintings and when he's depicting a pack of wolves ripping apart a carcass, you're thinking: it's a series of dots on the paper.

AR— Wit, or maybe humour, seems to be an important, and somewhat under-rated quality in art right now. Peter describes the 'Boulders, Rocks and Stones' series as being "like caricatures of rocks", for example. They're intrinsically funny as well as hugely serious, or monstrous on certain occasions. They've certainly an obvious 'rock-ness' about them and could

imaginary representations, on dreams and fantasies. What's more important than what places are like is what we want other places to mean. Alain de Botton's recent book 'The Art of Travel' is all about this. The way we imagine places is so much more interesting than their actual characteristics, which are always a let down and too specific.

DK — Peter remarked recently about having seen Nova Scotia, flying over it from a plane at 30,000 feet: "I knew I had to go there, but if I did, it would never compare to the fantasy I have of it. Your imagined view of the world is much stronger." I think everyone knows that feeling. His paintings of Montana are so simplified as to be almost an ur-landscape, like the kind a four-year old might conjure up if asked to draw a desert: big skies, bigger plains. All of the action becomes imperceptible: giant buffalo are specks in the distance. Without any details, anything too specific, your mind fills in the blanks.

AR— Also, Peter's paintings have an unexpected poetry, or find a poetry in the lacunae between describing things as you expect them and total abstraction. It's a poetry which comes from handling the medium in such a disarmingly straightforward way. He doesn't really employ any of the technical tricks you find elsewhere in contemporary art which are so seductive – photo-realist illusions, gestural finesse, hallucinatory detail, etc. It's also important that the poetics and politics are one; that the medium and the message are the same thing, in his work. His handling of materials and of paint stack up; and they convey his ideas in an incredibly particular way.

scarcely be anything else. But equally, they're about as far away materially from what they stand in for as could be possible, though incongruity doesn't really exhaust why they're smart and funny. Being fragile, lightweight, obviously hand-made, and constructed cheekily in a few minutes, rather than compressed over millennia means you read them in at least two ways at once and have to shuttle between the two (or more) to get to grips with them.

ST— Peter leaves space for our imagination to fill. His works are like the best games, which are always elementary ones – you're invited to let your imagination run riot. Each of his works seems free-form and without clear boundaries as to what you're supposed to 'do with them'.

AR— The rocks are, I think, the most unexpected way one could recreate an entire slice of the mythical mid-West. But they work. Paper, scissors, stone (as it were). Simple things, but you're hooked. The rocks seem, to me, to exemplify Peter's process, too: he manages to combine the comically absurd and the gently poetic in one work. He'd once said about them, "I like the labour-intensive repetitive process: it's like the reverse of being in prison; instead of breaking rocks, you're making them." It's such a great image. You can't really get more absurd than that.

MC— Much of Peter's work seems to me to be about conjuring a sense of place, through the most oblique means possible. Even the work 'Watches of Switzerland' – an anti-catalogue of all the watches made there – conjured up a type of place, or maybe why you wouldn't want to live there. I'd always thought that Peter was avoiding literal realism in order to underline how our relationship to 'elsewhere' is based on

ST — Rather than being overtly political in any didactic or earnest way, both images and objects are left open, almost unfinished so that we're drawn into seeing the world from his point of view rather than confronted abrasively. I remember he described wanting the Montana works to embody all the myths that America has to offer, whilst undermining them at the same time: "I wanted to paint a fantasy America. Like a story told in the eighth person. Like a Johnny Cash song. Like a film still. A tempting glimpse of something." And that's all you get.

MC— If his landscapes are about deferred desire, and the promise of an unattainable wilderness, I think the series of paintings he's been working on right now originate from the same impetus. These are the series of billboard-sized recreations of adverts for the Olympics, which are monumental of sorts (again), as they should be for such a global event. But the style is so anti-heroic, anti-monumental, that the myth just disappears, melts into thin air. Peter had said, "Just as wanting a really good television now is about desire and aspiration, the Olympics really is a kind of summit of physical achievement; they present an impossible dream." The works seem to continue Peter's quizzical unpicking of what are almost universally shared ideals and aspirations: that the Olympics are heroic, and the athletes are mortal gods.

ST— Do you think you could describe Peter's work as quintessentially British? What I'm thinking of is that I can see parallels between Peter's work and the British approach to sport. There is the great British attitude – but I don't know whether or not this is only a British thing – that it's the taking part that counts. In the last Olympics, for the Americans and Chinese it was clearly about the winning. As a nation, we seem to expect to be the best, but clearly aren't, and it's not necessarily through a lack of effort. We never seem to stop believing that next time, next time we'll be the winners, but the British mentality is always undermined by the attitude that winning isn't everything. Peter's work seems to echo this – he aspires to the qualities of the original object he recreates, but never succeeds. I find that aspiration incredibly beautiful; that the rain will stop and the sun will come out if you believe hard enough – it's not impossible, but the odds are stacked against you.

DK— I think the recent Olympic pieces also relate closely to, or come out of, the ongoing series of logotype paintings. They embody something of a brand, if that's the right word for the Olympics. I guess nobody sees it as a brand, though it is. The paintings reflect the eternal hope, that we all have, that perfection is possible, here physically. In terms of consumption, and the logotypes series, it's the idea that that investment in a product will bring you repleteness, or perfect completeness.

AR — The comedian Armando Iannucci said that there were only two moments of perfect happiness in life: Seeing a friend fail, and unwrapping a brand new CD. In a similar kind of way, both hope and disappointment are there in Peter's work. As he said: "In my paintings, you get something close to the immediate elation of having, say, a Cartier watch, but there's a disappointing shortfall because of the way my paintings are made." One of the reasons they're so is that he keeps both balls in the air at the same time, if you'll excuse the cliché.

ST— Personally, I love really nice things and I'm guilty of buying fashionable labels and dismissing unfashionable ones. You don't just buy a fashionable item, you buy self-confidence; the reassurance that you've purchased quality and you'll feel great. Peter's work is incredibly powerful in its ability to undermine those values, in quite a new and unexpected way, and in the way it draws attention to your own insecurities whilst doing so with a really engaging humour. Humour in art is an incredibly difficult thing – it normally boils down to thing being one line-gags, but in Peter's work it's integral and essential to every aspect of what he does.

HM— While the humour in Peter's work is obvious, it is possible to read an uglier, less utopian view of the world from the colonizing of the American 'wild west', to the avaricious and unnecessary consumption of branded goods. I say this knowing that I am a class-A hypocrite: I want, I have nice things, and I want more – whether a real Rolex watch or a painted one.

AR— The shows in 2004–5 are in galleries in cities as diverse as Sunderland, Belfast, Canterbury, Blackpool and Birmingham. I was curious as to the precise reasons why you as curators felt that his work was especially appropriate both to your spaces and audiences.

ST— I think it's especially appropriate to show Peter's work in Blackpool. I think that the concepts explored in Peter's work are very pronounced there. Blackpool, as a place, exists believing that it is possible of achieving anything; that it's the tallest and fastest the biggest and the best, when really it isn't. Rather it's beautifully amateurish. It's the embodiment of the entrepreneurial dream, but rather than being built with the recognized ingredients for success, it's stuck together with sticky-tape. It instills personality where multi-national corporations rigorously sanitize. There is a shop here called 'Steals', which is an odd name for a shop anyway, but the sign outside reads, 'There's No Place Like This Place, Anywhere Near This Place, So This Must Be The Place'. Now that could be one of Peter's titles – he's got an exceptional eye for isolating what's absurd about the claims that manufacturers make. And at underlining how ridiculous, inflated, or inconsequential they usually are. Where Peter's work draws attention to its own inadequacies, Blackpool carries on its business as though it were blissfully unaware that Las Vegas really exists, or of any of the kinds of regeneration that other British city centres have recently undertaken. That's its incredible charm as a place, but it's an unconscious one.

MC— I'd found Peter's way of working with particular spaces incredibly engaging. The show at the Italian Cultural Institute, for example, created a whole environment in a way which you least expected and in a place where you'd least expect that kind of work. And yet the means he uses to create an environment, a situation rather than a single autonomous object, was almost barely visible, barely there. It's difficult to

The world is open for business, 2003

A camera for the computer age, 2003

tell, too, at what point an object stops being an object and becomes an installation, or part of something larger. By which I mean that you were overwhelmed by the scale and strangeness of the boulders, rocks and stones series whilst almost being underwhelmed at the same time – an odd kind of compound sensation. Peter's work is monumental without being monumental, formalistic of sorts without being formalist, and clearly informed by a critical intelligence that doesn't bludgeon you into submission. That level of lightness of touch is quite rare, and is ideal for the Herbert Read space which is part of an educational institution. Peter's ability to communicate both in and outside the gallery, to engage with the institution on a number of levels, is also important.

HM— My interest in showing Peter's work in Belfast stems from the very positive response to his work in 'Perspective' in 2001. In fact 'Perspective' comes with an award of £6,000, and when Peter didn't win it that year a reviewer claimed in print that "Playful Peter wuz robbed in OBG contest" so I guess I owe him one. Seriously though, Peter is one of the most prolific and constantly strong artists I know. I was excited about the potential narrative he could create using the range of spaces we have available at OBG.

DK— *Previously for Ikon Peter had created a 'multiple-performance' called 'Hotdog Stall' in 2000, and this seems like an ideal opportunity to build upon that by creating a series of events over the summer of 2005. I like the idea that everyone has access to his works in different ways, and the variety of ideas he develops and the diversity of means of communicating them is incredibly open-ended, democratic. Whether we realise a falconry display in the centre of Birmingham, or distribute a compilation CD, the work will be available to audiences who wouldn't normally engage with art, as well as to artists and more specialist audiences. These off-site works*

reflect site-specificity, a direct connection to a place and its context and mark an unselfconsciousness that lies in contrast to the usual perceptions of public art as something often static, awkward and out dated. Peter's work in contrast, evokes a romantic and mythical intervention to the generic urban environment. By introducing more ephemeral proposals such as sound and performance his work becomes more dynamic and vital.

Many of his signature themes are explored such as otherworldliness, myth and play. In the audio work 'Howling Wolves', Peter re-creates the distant cries of a pack of wild animals announcing their dawn arrival in the deserted city streets thus bringing to mind a far away place. As ever, there is a tongue-in-cheek suggestion, here that the inhabitants of the natural world can be just as menacing as any urban dweller. Broadcast from a roving vehicle the cries could be rather alarming, yet despite this, they seem strangely familiar and reassuring. Continuing with his obsession around the notion of artifice Peter proposes to install an enormous inflatable carcass in a public square, reminiscent of an archaeological dig. This Disney-esque public sculpture made from rubber is, as with all these works, an occasion to provide people with conversational material about myth. These off-site projects will be read by different people in different ways, but Peter's work is so generous, so complex in its range of references, that everyone could have some initial engagement with it.

AR— The title of Peter's show in Sunderland, 'What You'd Expect', seems to exemplify that. Naturally it's borrowed from a corporate slogan, which underlines how crazy the ideas and dreams we're sold actually are, but it does other things too – it challenges you to disagree with it, but without being confrontational or difficult. And it asks you to laugh at it, without being flippant. It gently prods you, saying – what exactly did you expect anyway?

PROPOSLA FOR DEBBIE KERMODE AT THE IKON GALLERY, BIRMINGHAM
FOR THE OFFSITE PROJECTS PROGRAMME 2005.
July 2004.

I propose to install large oversize inflatable carcasses
(based on sculptures of the same name) in the main square
and around Birmingham. The carcasses would be placed so
that youg could walk around and through them. The
carcasses would want to be 30 to 40 feet tall and
would be constructed from the same material as children's
boncy castles, they would be inflated by silent compressors.
It would be good if the carcasses wod arrive at the pre-
arranged location early in the day and then are inflated
quickly so that people can chance upon them as they go about
their day-to-day routines. I'd also like to see them in the
park.

BIRMINGHAM

Birmingham

PROPOSAL FOR DEBBIE KERMODE AT THE IKON GALLERY, BIRMINGHAM
FOR THE OFFSITE PROJECTS PROGRAMME 2005.
June 2004

I propose to have the Midland's Falconry Display team
perform in the centre of Birmingham. The display would
take place on a Saturday. It would be advertised by
fliers, adverts in shop windows and through inserts
in local newspapers.
I would hope to have large birds of prey so that their
scale could be felt by all those who witness the event.
The birds would be displayed (whilst not in flight) in
cages and smaller display areas (perhaps a handling/petting
areas?) These would be constructed using unplaned timber
and strong garden netting.
If possible it would be good to do more than one display
during the day.

PROPOSAL FOR DEBBIE KERMODE AT THE IKON GALLERY, BIRMINGHAM
FOR THE OFFSITE PROJECTS PROGRAMME 2005.
june 2004.

I propose to play the recording of wolves howling, late at
night, in the centre of the city.
The recording could come from: essential horror sound effects
volume I.
The sound would come from a large bank of speakers housed
in the back of a hire van, so that it could be mobile. I
imagine the sound echoing round the streets and off the buildings
in the centre of town.
I think this should take place at the time of pub and/or
club closing time. It might also be good to do it very
early in the morning whilst the city is quiet.

BIRMINGHAM

Birmingham

AUDEMARS PIGUET
The master watchmaker

BAUME & MERCIER
GENÈVE

BLANCPAIN

BREITLING
1884

Breguet
Depuis 1775

Cartier

Chopard
GENÈVE

EBEL
the architects of time

FRANCK MULLER
GENÈVE

MANUFACTURE
GIRARD-PERREGAUX
DEPUIS 1791

GUCCI
TIMEPIECES

IWC
International Watch Co. Ltd. Schaffhausen
Since 1868

JAEGER-LECOULTRE

LONGINES
L'ÉLÉGANCE DU TEMPS DEPUIS 1832

OMEGA
The sign of excellence.

ORIS
Made in Switzerland
Since 1904

PATEK PHILIPPE
GENÈVE

PIAGET

RAYMOND WEIL
GENÈVE

TAGHeuer

VACHERON CONSTANTIN
Genève, depuis 1755

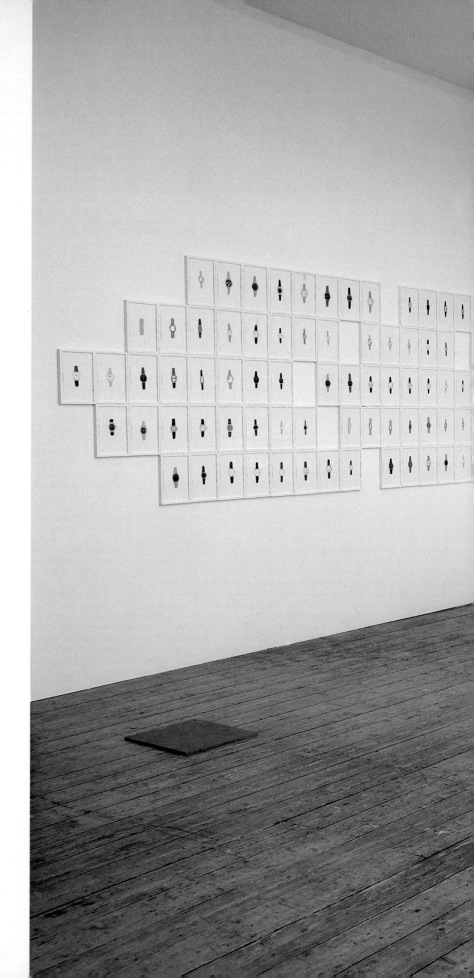

Previous pages and top left: *Watches of Switzerland,* Installation. 169 framed drawings, seven sculptures,
wall drawing, dimensions variable. Richard Salmon Gallery, 2003. *Private collection, California*

This page and left: Adverts installed at *Brand New and Retro,* The Empire, London. 2004

Far left centre: Adverts installed at *Through the Window,* Italian Cultural Institute, London. 2003

Far left bottom: *Paintings and Sculpture,* installed at Rare, New York, 2001.

Various constructions. 2001–04. Card, hot-glue, plastic, cotton, wood, acrylic

It's almost uncanny the remarkable timing of your Thai hostess. It seems she knows what you want before you know yourself. 2000 (detail). *Private collection, New York.*

We take more care of you. 2000. *Government Art Collection*

Hertz hire keys. 2002 / Cigarette lighter. 2002

Cartier, Paris. 2001

Tomorrow, today. 30 September 2001. Dia. 31.5cm. Acrylic, MDF

The link between the past and the future. 4 October 2001. 14.3 x 17.5cm. Spray paint, perspex, acrylic

Now you can change your environment without changing your tyres. 1999

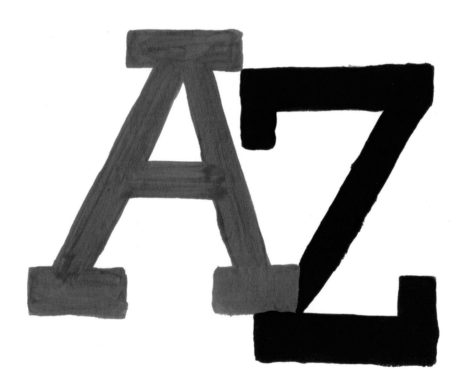

The A–Z from the London A–Z. 2003

1st

Grand Prix
de France
1979

50 YEARS

Beechcraft

1932 — 1982

Mobile executives have an immediate advantage. 2000

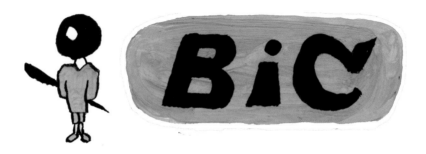

Ferrari

Ferrari, the dancing horse. 2003

FONDÉ EN 1848

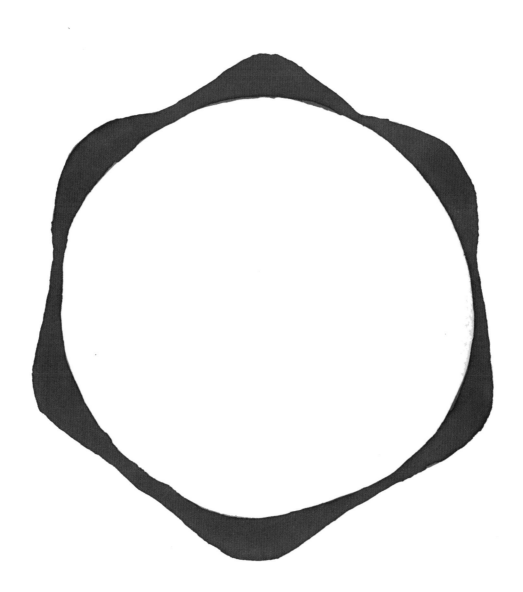

Gorna bania – bottled at source. 2004

PATEK
PHILIPPE

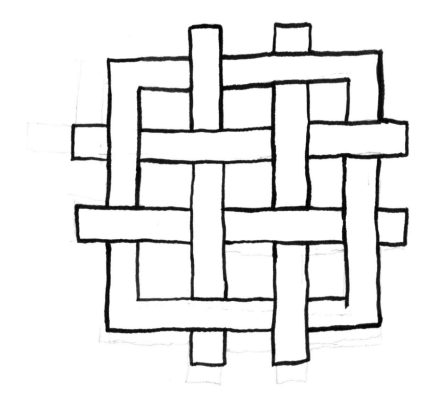

A cure for cancer might be just out of our reach. 2003

Cartier

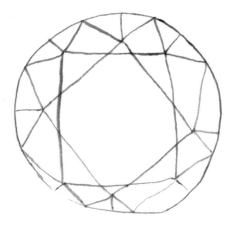

A Tiffany diamond. 2003

Tinta rojo. 2004

British
airways

A new vision. 2000

When you shoot for perfection use perfection. 2000

We have a history of keeping you ready for any photo opportunity. 1998

No one cares more about your image than Nikon. 2004

Sansui – we explode! 2001

Would you believe it... A digital harpsichord. 2001

Schwan Stabilo Universal. 2004

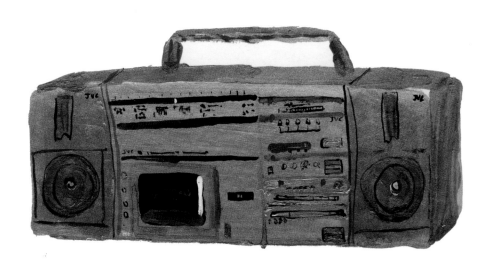

Reliability is a major reason why JVC is an industry leader. 2000

The sure sign of innovation. 2001

Technology that conquered Hollywood. 2001

Preserving more than just memories. 2001

Pet, pest, appetiser. 2003

A reference in complete simplicity. 2003

Start running. 2001

Montreal 1976

Worldwide Sponsor

1988 Olympic Games

TV/Audio

The sure sign of innovation. 2003

We are United. 2003

Peter Liversidge & The Aesthetic of the Artist's Multiple

Text: Stephen Bury

The artist's multiple is made by an artist; there is usually more than one, with the denial of the authentic 'original' and the insistence on the equality of each one in the edition being important considerations; and the artist chooses the medium 'artist's multiple' rather than painting, sculpture, photography, film or video (although the multiple might take the form of one or all of these). Then, there is an inner core definition: the artist's multiple should be in an edition of at least 50; it would be fabricated by another; it would use new materials and processes in its manufacture; it would simulate an every-day object but not be useful; and it would be humorous in its subversion of that object. Object too implies three rather than two dimensions. And, lastly, mail art could be seen as merely a mode of distribution (and exhibition) of the multiple.

How do Peter Liversidge's multiples measure up to these criteria? The Duchampian test – one is unique, two is a pair, three is mass produced – is probably a paraphrase of his more philosophical statement that "one is unity, two is double, duality, and three is the rest." Certainly, Liversidge's first multiples, the 'SOS' badge in an edition of 100, and 'Bird Box' in an edition of 500 (shown at his degree show at Exeter), are in the fifty plus category:

they were also unsigned and unnumbered. 'Bird Box' of 1996, consists of a die-cut cardboard self-assembly bird-box, complete with a wooden perch, previous works shredded for a nest lining, and an artificial robin; it was also a mail art work in the sense that its 'owner' was intended to photograph, draw or document its new location and return this documentation to the 'artist'. But other multiples have ranged in edition size – from 3, to 10, 14, 20, even up to 500. The determination of a particular size may vary from the over-determined logic of the title of 'One 14th of Darth Vader', 1998, i.e. there are 14 of these, to the marketing decisions of the Multiple Store for 'Interstate' and 'Interstate II', 2002, in editions of 10 and 100 respectively.

Often the inspiration for a multiple may arise from the studio 'jeu d'esprit', or artistic playfulness. Like Picasso's 'Pomme', 1909–10, a crudely carved wooden apple that references Picasso's own cubist still-lives and those of Cézanne, but which was never actually cast in bronze, Liversidge's multiples often start as a prototype in the studio: some may develop into editioned multiples and others not for various reasons. To complicate things further, some one-off pieces have the 'aura' of the multiple: in his joint show with Antonio Riello at the Italian Cultural Institute,

London, 2003–4, Liversidge exhibited 'Cartier, Paris', a rather distasteful piece of jewellery in a red jewel case, made from card, hot glue, cotton and acrylic. This is a one-off piece, but it could be seen as a unique multiple, if that is not a contradiction in terms. In the same series, Liversidge's other hot-glued 'constructions' included Hitachi, Leica, Olympus, and Kodak cameras; a Minolta flash unit; a Philips pocket memo all of 2001–03. Is each individual piece a multiple? Another piece in the exhibition, 'Boulders, Rocks & Stones', 2002 and ongoing, made from masking tape and bubble-wrap, invites each individual component to be considered as a multiple part of a whole, and provokes speculation about how, in some sort of sorites, a piling up of multiples, it suddenly becomes magically complete at a certain point. There are further connections with other pieces in his body of work. The 'Watches of Switzerland' installation of 169 separately framed works on paper depicts the entire contents of a catalogue of luxury timepieces. Exhibited in 'The West' at the Richard Salmon Gallery in May–July 2003, it could also be construed as a whole made from 'multiple' parts.

Nor is the question of fabrication any less complicated. The constructivist admiration of fabrication, as in Laszlo Moholy-Nagy's 'Telephone Pictures', 1922, which were ordered and specified down the telephone to a sign factory with graph paper and the factory's colour chart at both ends, joined with the ambition of conceptual art, where for LeWitt an idea is 'a machine that makes art'. Liversidge's 'Proposals for Paul E. Stolper and Jason Brown for the Cab Gallery: Reg: S310 DGJ Model Tx:1', 1999, was (originally) a mail art project, an artist's book, an artist's multiple for the passenger seat shelf of the taxi, a recipe book for installations in that space. This is at the LeWitt end of the fabrication project. At the other end of things, 'Interstate' adopts the emphasis on professional fabrication identified with the Multiple Store editions. '24 Hours', a mail art project and multiple, depended on Liversidge's discovery and use of a retired letterpress printer.

One of the deciding points of when a prototype should go on to be a multiple, remain unborn or be a one-off sculpture, centres on the question whether the artist needs to be involved in its making and editioning, and this also affects the edition size, although the artist can sometimes cast himself as the fabricator. But once again, the situation is not clear cut. One of Liversidge's own favourite multiples is 'Objects Made At Work Whilst I Should've Been Working', 1997–99, in an edition of 4. Here the handmade-ness and artist's time and skill subvert the framing factory fabrication process: "I realized how much time was actually taken up at work, when I wanted to be working in the studio. I started making the objects to try and reclaim some of the time spent working. All the objects were small enough to be hidden quickly up a sleeve or in a short top pocket, and like scrimshaw work they were made from available materials; found off-cuts of wood and fashioned by the available tools and sandpaper. Each object took days, sometimes weeks to complete, using only the time made available whilst at work."

This is resistance to the artist's use of fabrication, the division of labour which characterizes the artist's multiple. The materials that Liversidge uses seem largely to conform with the expectations that the multiple should be made from new materials and through novel processes – we have hot glue, bubble wrap, masking tape, stove enamel, acrylic, aluminium, reflective materials, helium balloons etc. It comes as a bit of a shock to come to the bronze of 'Door Stop', 2000. So it is perhaps all the more surprising that the work came about in part through a conversation with myself. After being approached to take a job in New York, I had flippantly and in rhetorical inversion, remarked that 'as one door opens, another door shuts'; and 'Door Stop' was Liversidge's response. The translation of the humble, quotidian door stop, complete with its banal self-inscription 'door wedge', was 360 degree cast by Liversidge in an edition of 50, using the most popular patination colour available.

Above: Objects made at work whilst I should've been working. (Ear Plugs) 1997–99. 1.9 x 1cm dia.

Below: Untitled (earth edition). Ed.10, 1999 0.5 x 0.5cm dia. Map pin, Acrylic paint

For the multiple, bronze has been something of a taboo medium, too redolent of editioned sculpture, like the serried heads of Giambologna. And my core definition of the multiple had demanded 'it would use new materials and processes rather, than for example, traditional bronze.' The translation of the humble, quotidian door stop, complete with its banal self-inscription 'door wedge', was cast by Liversidge in an edition of 50, in standard bronze.

The usual hard rubber has flexibility enough to be easily used as a door stop. The bronze version could just about (but very awkwardly) be used to prop open a door, but its functionality is undermined by its costliness — a sort of comic version of 'Family Circle' columnist Vicki Lansky's 'Another use for… 101 Common Household Items'. And it is this subversion or literal impropriety that provides a humorous thrust to much of Liversidge's work. The Cab Gallery projects proposal of 2000 for a windscreen vinyl strip, typically proclaiming the inseparableness and undying love of a couple — Dante and Laura, Abelard and Heloise, Brett and Sharon — is subverted with Liversidge's version: Jason and Meter. On the other hand, the 'Mind the Gap' proposal was for the inscription of the familiar London Underground

announcement at Holborn and other stations, warning the passenger of the gap between the compartment and the platform, on the taxi cab carpet by the door.

These are conceptually inappropriate readings of one area of experience onto another. It is at its most effective when reinforced by material inappropriateness. 'The Perfect Match', 1996, made for the '9x' show at the Tannery, London, itself conjoins football studs with a slipper, suggesting the incongruity of armchair watchers of football on 'Match of the Day'. And here again the aesthetic of the artist's multiple transfers across to some of Liversidge's one-off works. 'The Quiet Luxury of Rolls Royce', 1998, shown at the A22 Projects Gallery consists of a roughly sliver-painted logo of the eponymous luxury car manufacturer. The medium is a torn, ancient and fragile section of (presumably) a wooden package case in an imminent state of total disintegration: the contrast of the reputed solidity and reliability of the brand with this manifestation is a telling one.

Traditionally — if the artist's multiple has a tradition — the multiple has been seen as three rather than two-dimensional. In the real world, most things are three dimensional — even paper has a width. But it was Joseph Beuys's work in the 1970s

and 1980s with multiples as photographs, film, drawings and prints as well as sculptural objects that placed more of the emphasis on the intention of the artist rather on any particular medium, such an aesthetic perhaps reaching its apogee with Ben Vautier's 'multiple by label' idea in his 'A Total Work of Art', where anyone could add the label to any object, endowing upon it the status of a work of art. Liversidge's multiples spread across the two- / three-dimensional divide: the 'SOS' Badge, 'Interstate' and 'Interstate II', the 'I Love the North Montana Plains' T-shirt, the poster from 'The West' exhibition at the Richard Salmon Gallery, 2003, the '24 Days' folded cards, wrapped in brown paper of 1999 are on the two-dimensional end of the spectrum; whilst 'Bird Box', 1996, the football-studded 'The Perfect Match', 1996, 'Door Stop', 2000, 'Objects Made At Work While I Should Have Been Working', 1998, the cup and saucer set of 'Another 24 Hours on the North Montana Plains', 2000, are more emphatically three-dimensional. Somewhere in between the two are the demarcating signs, fences and bunting.

Nor does the object being primarily two- or three-dimensional affect whether Liversidge chooses to distribute it via mail art. Although, '24 Days', 1999, 'Addresses', 1999 and ongoing, and 'I Have @ Mail Box' of 2000, were obviously mail outs, for his Spacex Gallery show in 1995 Liversidge sent a whole chair, joint by joint, stamped and addressed through the Post Office, whilst the very object-like 'Bird Box' needed to be completed by the recipient who would send a photograph or drawing back to the artist. Liversidge seems to enjoy being able to send 'abnormal' objects through the post, implicating the quotidian postman in his enterprises.

All this reinforces a 'read across' of the aesthetic of the artist's multiple over the whole range of Liversidge's work: his use of the two-dimensional multiple undermines the traditional hegemony of painting; sculptures and paintings are assembled in series, suggesting the multi-part multiple; new materials and processes extend well beyond his multiple output. Liversidge sees himself primarily as first and foremost as an artist rather than as a painter, sculptor or artist's-multiples maker: an idea leads to a prototype which might be the art work or lead to another incarnation, or the idea may be abandoned for ever or at least until it becomes technically or economically feasible.

In the last few years the location of both the artwork and the artist's multiple in Liversidge's work has been interestingly

and creatively unstable and problematic. The series of performance multiples — the mustard and tomato-sauced 'Hotdog', first performed at the A22 Gallery, where the hotdog cardboard packaging was or could be signed and numbered; 'Ice Cream', 2003 and 'Kebabsha', 2004 for various locations during the British Council touring show, 'Multiplication' highlight this. In retrospect these 'performance multiples' are reminiscent of the happenings and multiples of Claes Oldenburg's 'Store', but perhaps with a greater sense of the ephemeral — the hotdog, kebab or ice cream are consumed and cease to be in the world. Fast food becomes a fast multiple — there may be left a signed and numbered package or a photograph or video of the event, but where does the multiple or artwork lie: in the conception, the performance of the production and consumption of the food, its packaging (by now a less than pristine container) or its documentation? Is the multiple here a prop or product? Is the documentation the artwork?

The late 1960s and 1970s aesthetic of the dematerialization of the art object, which Lucy Lippard characterized in 1973 as "a deemphasis on material aspects (uniqueness, permanence, decorative attractiveness)" and her insistence that

"a piece of paper is as much an object, or as 'material' as a ton of lead", also challenged the gallery system and the concomitant production of art objects for commercial exchange within it. Liversidge's 'Hotdog Stand', 2004, was a day-long performance in a car park off Brick Lane in Whitechapel, which saw what could be called a 'remnant' multiple sale, which rapidly escalated (or deteriorated) into barter. Objects were swopped for a helping hand when it came to packing up, or for a short call on a mobile phone. These exchanges were also documented by photography, but just as much an object as anything else in our three dimensional world: cut an object in half and you get another surface.

The final paradox of Liversidge's activities with the artist's multiples (or his multiple activities) is this movement towards the de-materialized, whilst longing for the carefully and lovingly crafted object, such as 'Objects Made At Work Whilst I Should've Been Working', 1997–99, where the finely sanded but useless objects are housed with all the care that might be lavished on expensive cigars. And when the object is absent or diffused over an installation or performance, Liversidge's deep and powerful respect for the object enriches its absence.

Top: Bird Box. Ed. 500, 1996. Cardboard, hot-glue, shredded photocopies of previous work, wood, false robin, instructions. *The London Institute Collection*

Snowball. Ed.11,1999. Dia 7cm
Tennis ball, acrylic paint. *Czech Museum of Fine Art, Prague*

Brick. (Maquette) unlimited edition, 2001-2004
10.5 x 24 x 7.5cm. Cardboard, hot-glue

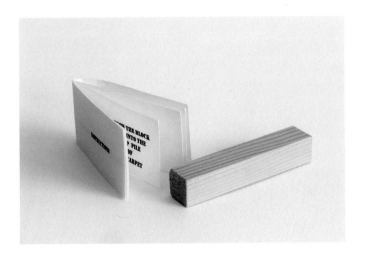

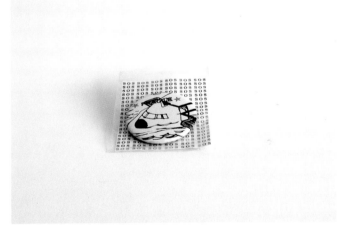

Block of wood to place in a deep pile carpet to make walking in shoes with thin soles uneven. Ed. 50, 1998. Dimensions variable
Plastic case, instruction booklet, wood

Door stop. Ed. 50, 2000. 13.6 x 4.3 x 2.6cm. Bronze

Dust edition. Ed. 20. 28 March 1998. Jar: 3.8 x dia 3.5cm. Label: 9.4 x 4.7cm
Glass jar; containing dust collected from a gallery floor in Dublin, stickers, black cotton, label

The perfect match. Ed.22, 1996
Size 9 carpet slippers, football studs

Brush for David Dellafiora. Ed 5, 1998. 28.6 x 9.7 x 6cm
Field Study Collection, Australia

SOS badge. Ed. 100 (unnumbered), 1995. Dia. 5.6cm
Badge, photocopied airplane emergency instructions

MONTANA
FOREVER!!

The usurper of the North has failed in his efforts to enslave the freemen of Montana.

The wives and daughters of Montana will be saved from the brutality of his soldiers.

Now is the time to emigrate to the big sky of America.

A free passage, and ~~~~ und, is offered at Salt Lake City to all applicants. Every sett~~~~ es a location of

FIFTEEN HUNDRED ACRES OF LAND

On the 23rd of February, a force of 1000 came in sight of Great Falls, and on the 25th General Roseaud arrived at that place with 2500 more men, and demanded surrender of the fort held by 150 Montanians, and on refusal, he attempted storm the fort, twice, with his whole force, but was repelled with the loss 723 men and the Montanians lost none. Many of his troops, the Liberals of Alberta are brought on to Montana in irons and are urged forward with the promise of the women and plunder of Montana.

The Montanian forces were marching to relieve Great Falls on March 2nd. The Government of Montana is supplied with plenty of arms, ammunition, animals, provisions, parcels, &~~~~

Opposite Page: Montana Forever! Ed.100, 2003. 29.5 x 41.5cm. Screen print, each individually 'aged'. *Private Collection, London*

Another 24 hours on the North Montana Plains. Ed.10. Ceramic coffee cups

Above: Interstate. Ed.10, 2001. Sign 146 x 25.4cm, poles 110cm x 8cm dia 3mm aluminium, stovepipe enamel, reflective material, fixings. *Multiple Store*

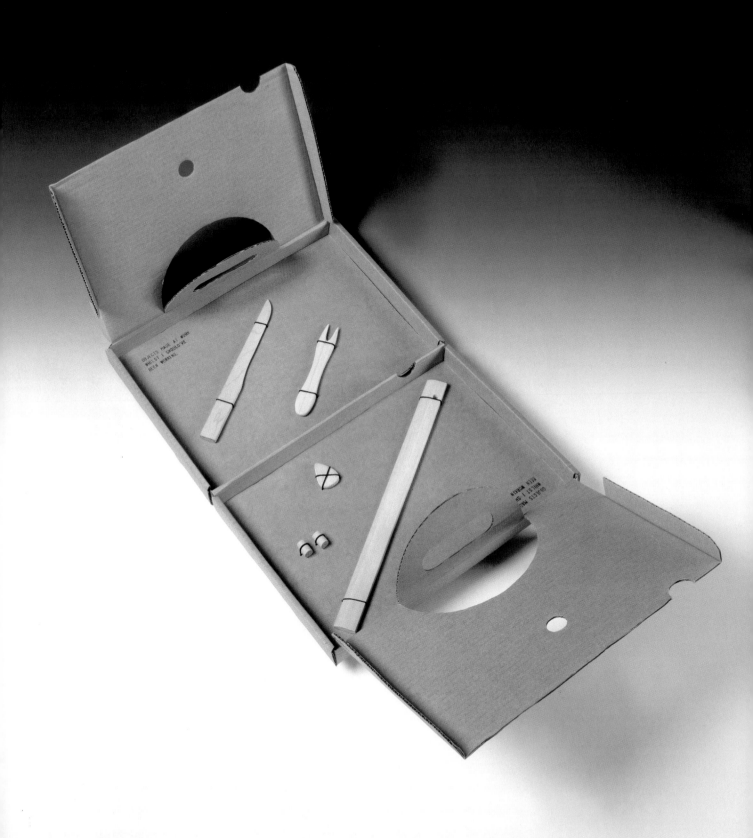

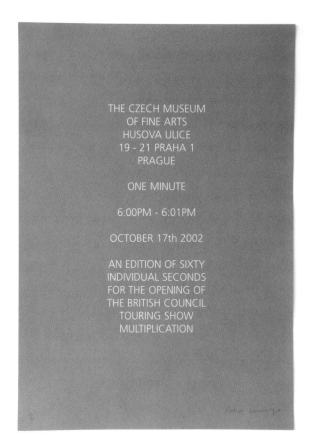

THE CZECH MUSEUM
OF FINE ARTS
HUSOVA ULICE
19 - 21 PRAHA 1
PRAGUE

ONE MINUTE

6:00PM - 6:01PM

OCTOBER 17th 2002

AN EDITION OF SIXTY
INDIVIDUAL SECONDS
FOR THE OPENING OF
THE BRITISH COUNCIL
TOURING SHOW
MULTIPLICATION

Above: One Hundred and twenty minutes. Ed. 60, 2004. 104 x 77.5cm
Stock paper, screen print. Distributed to mark the lecture given at the
National Gallery of Tirana, Albania, 21st September 2004. *British Council*

Opposite page: Objects made at work whilst I should've been working.
1997–99. Ed. 4. Dimensions variable. Obeche, Maple, Poplar and Tulip wood,
cardboard, elastic, label. *British Council*

Above: One minute (An edition of sixty seconds). Ed. 60, 2002. 59.6 x 42cm
Screen printed poster. Distributed to mark the first sixty seconds
of a lecture given at the Czech Museum of Fine Arts, Prague.
17 October 2002 at 6pm. *British Council*

An Edition of Twentyfive   Peter Liversidge 10th November 2000

Hotdog performance. 1998– ongoing. Stand, hotdogs, buns, editioned serving tray
Opposite page: Montana placards. 2004. Photocopies, MDF, cable ties

Icecream performance. Ed. 50, 2003. Stand, icecream, editioned paper tubs. Ljubljana, Slovenia. *British Council*

Kebabsha performance. Ed. 50, 2004. Stand, kebabsha, editioned serving tray. Sofia, Bulgaria. *British Council*

AIR MAIL
PAR AVION

39 Seconds

MAR 20 2000

00144/1000 ‖‖‖‖‖‖‖‖‖‖‖‖‖‖‖‖‖‖‖‖‖‖‖‖‖‖

Peter Liversidge 1999

CASSIE HOWARD
24 MUSEUM HOUSE
BURNHAM STREET
BETHNAL GREEN
LONDON
E2 OJA

UNITED KINGDOM

CASSIE HOWARD
24 MUSEUM HOUSE
BURNHAM STREET
BETHNAL GREEN
LONDON
E2 OJA

Peter Liversidge 2000

Ms CASSIE HOWARD
24 MAISON de MUSEE
RUE de BURNHAM
BETHNAL VERT
LONDRES
E2 OJA
ANGLETERRE

Peter Liversidge 2000

CASSIE HOWARD
24 MUSEUM HUIS
BURNHAM STRAAT
BETHNAL GROEN
LONDEN
E2 OJA
GROOT - BRITTANNIË

Peter Liversidge 2000

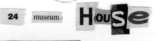

CASSIE HOWARD
24 MUSEUM HOUSE
BURNHAM STREET
BETHNAL GREEN
LONDON
E2 OJA

Peter Liversidge, 2000

Peter Liversidge 2001

Addresses. 1999– ongoing. 10 ply printers card

Peter Liversidge 2001

Peter Liversidge 2001

Peter Liversidge 2001

Peter Liversidge 2001

Peter Liversidge 2003

Missent by ...
CASSIE HOWARD
FLAT ONE
180 GROVE ROAD
BOW   E3 5TG
LONDON

44/2000   H.K.   Peter Liversidge 2003

CASSIE HOWARD
COLD HALL LODGE
Kiln Road
NORTH WEALD
EPPING
ESSEX   CM16 6AD
england

Peter Liversidge 2003

CASSIE HOWARD
Flat 1 180
Grove
Road Bow
E3 5TG   UK

Peter Liversidge 2004

Royal Mail De Dd Cymru   SE Wales
06.05.04

CASSIE HOWARD
FLAT 1
180 GROVE ROAD
BOW
LONDON
E3 5TG.

Peter Liversidge 2004

CASSIE HOWARD
FLAT 1
180 GROVE ROAD
BOW
LONDON
E3 5TG

Peter Liversidge 2004

CASHSHIE HOWARDH
FLATH 1
180 GROVE RRUGH
bow
LONDER
E3 5TG
ANGLI

Peter Liversidge 2004

Opposite page:
I have @ mail box. Unnumbered ed. 250, 1999. 10.4 x 15.8cm
In the bleak mid-winter months very little stirs on the North Montana Plains. Unnumbered ed. 500, 2000
Darkness is the cover for all kinds of evil on the North Montana Plains. Unnumbered ed. 500, 2001
All 10 ply printers card. *The Bremham Collection, London*

I have @ mail box

In the bleak mid - winter months
very little stirs on the
North Montana Plains

Darkness is the cover for
all kinds of evil on the
North Montana Plains

Peter Liversidge Solo Exhibitions

2005— *What You'd Expect*
Northern Gallery for Contemporary Art, Sunderland
Ormeau Baths Gallery, Belfast
Herbert Read Gallery, Kent Insitute of Art & Design
The Grundy Art Gallery, Blackpool
Ikon Gallery, Birmingham (offsite projects)

2004— *The Secret Knowledge of the Back Roads*
Paul Stolper, London

2003— *Western Country*, RARE, New York
The West, Richard Salmon Gallery, London

2001— *Paintings and Sculpture*, RARE, New York

2000— *Peter Liversidge*, From Space, Manchester
The North Montana Plains, Cairn Gallery, Nailsworth,
Gloustershire

1999— *Paintings and Sculpture*, A22 Projects, London
Paintings and Mail art, Timothy Everest, London

1998— *Paintings and Multiples*, A22 Projects, London

Selected Group Exhibitions

2004— *Brand New and Retro*, UP Projects, London
Landscape? #2, Towner Gallery, Eastbourne
Ain't No Love in the Heart of the City, curated by
Gordon Dalton, CBAT Gallery, Cardiff

2003— *Through the window*, Italian Cultural Institute, London
Kabinett der Abstrakten, curated by Goshka Macuga,
Bloomberg Space, London
Work, Floating IP, Manchester, curated by Dave Beech
and Rachel Goodyear
*Living with art: Drawing and Paintings from the Evans
Collection*, Rivington Gallery, London

2002— *Surface*, 181 Offord Road, London
Deluxe, Sala Plaza de Espana, Madrid, and tour
Guns and Roses, 86 Brick Lane, London
Tricky Adios, K.S. Art, 73 Leonard Street, New York
Adapt now, Kelvingrove Museum, Glasgow
Cab Gallery Retrospective 1999—2001, Essor project
space, London

2001— *Multiplication*, British Council touring exhibition.
National Museum of Art, Bucharest
Perspective 2001, Ormeau Baths Gallery, Belfast
Record collection, Forde Espace d'art Contemporain,
Geneva, and tour
The Multiple Store at Roche Court, The New Art Centre,
Roche Court, Salisbury
Beautiful Productions, Whitechapel Gallery, London
Club, Beaconsfield, London
Le Confort Modern, Poitiers, France
Verbal-inter-visual, Leathaby Galleries, London
Dog-leg, 27 Guildhall Street, Northhampton
Desire and Pursuit of the Whole, Museum of St. Petersburg,
St. Petersburg
Insider Trading, The Manderville Hotel, London
Funny, Andrew Mummery Gallery, London

2000— *John Moores 21*, Walker Art Gallery, Liverpool
Better Scenery, two-person show / Adam Chodzko. Pand
Paulus Gallery, Schiedam, Holland
Arcade, Ikon Touring, Ikon Gallery, Birmingham and tour
Mul-te-ple-sho, A22 Projects, London
The Equinox, Cairn Gallery, Nailsworth, Gloustershire

1999— *Multiples and Editions*, ICA, London
Cab Gallery, London

Bibliography

2003— 'British Artists at Work' Gemma de Cruz, Amanda Eliasch,
Assouline Publishing 2003
Louisa Buck 'what's on' *The Art Newspaper*, N°138 Jul
Richard Dyer 'Highlights, London' *Contemporary*, May/Jun
Jessica Lack 'Exhibition preview' *Guardian Guide*, May 29
Jessica Lack 'Pick of the Week' *Guardian G2*, Jun 2

2002— 'Multiplication', Dr Stephen Bury, British Council 2002
'Artists Multiples and Editions' Steve Bury,
Ashgate Publishing, 2003.
Fisun Gunter, 'Guns and Roses', *Metro*, Jul 17
Mason Klien, *ArtForum*, Feb
Tim & Frantiska Gilman-Seveik, *Flash Art*, Jan/Feb

2001— 'Proposals for David Wilkinson and Annie Fletcher'
Ormeau Baths Gallery 2001
Village Voice, *Visual Arts*, Nov
'Text book Visual Art', Aidain Dunne, *Irish Times*,
Visual Arts, Oct 8
'Perspective 2001', Ian Hill, *Belfast Telegraph*, Sep 10
'Perspective 2001', Gavin Weston, *The Sunday Times* Oct 7
'The Top Ten', Charlotte Edwards, *Art Review*, Oct
'Multiples', Mark Harris, *Art Monthly*, May
'Cab-Gallery' *i-D*, Apr
'Funny review', Martin Herbert, *Time Out*, Jan 10—17

2000— 'Art London' Martin Coomer, 2000
'New British Art', Talious Somomat, November
'Cab-Gallery', Louisa Buck, *Evening Standard*, Nov 7
'Mul-te-ple-sho', Dr. Stephen Bury, *Art Monthly*, Jul
The Independent, Mark Chilvers, Jan 20

1999— *The Independent on Sunday*, Duncan Maclaren, Nov 22
'Cab Gallery', *Metro*, Nov 30
'Cab Gallery', Martin Coomer, *Time Out*, Nov 24—Dec 1
'Collected by the Famous', Ria Higgins, *Sunday Times
Magazine*, Nov 11
'Cab-Gallery', Louisa Buck, *The Art Newspaper*, N°97
'After Sensation', Marin Herbert, *Square Meal*, Aug
'Multiples', Jonathan Blond, *Art Review*, Jul
'Mail-Art', John Windsor, *The Independent magazine*, May 22

1998   Time Out, Martin Herbert, Nov 2—Dec 8
'Visual Arts', John Windsor, *The Independent*, Nov 22

Works in Permanent Collections

Government Art Collection, London
British Council Collection, London
British Library, London
Tate Gallery Archive, London
Towner Gallery, Eastbourne
Czech Museum of Fine Art, Prague
The London Institute Collection, London
The Bremham Collection, London
The Library Collection, University of Plymouth
Unilever, London

Allstate, you're in good hands, 2004